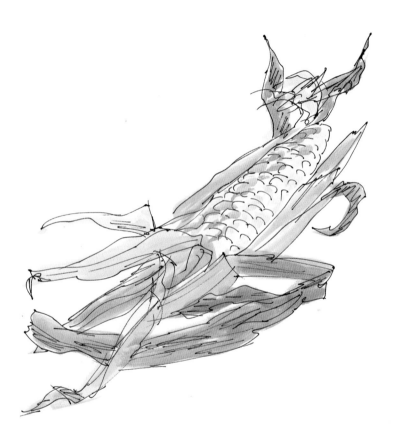

SWEET CORN

POEMS
BY JAMES
STEVENSON

WITH ILLUSTRATIONS
BY THE AUTHOR

GREENWILLOW
BOOKS,
NEW YORK

Watercolor paints and a black pen
were used for the full-color art.

Copyright © 1995 by
James Stevenson
All rights reserved. No part of this
book may be reproduced or utilized
in any form or by any means,
electronic or mechanical, including
photocopying, recording, or by any
information storage and retrieval
system, without permission in
writing from the Publisher,
Greenwillow Books, a division of
William Morrow & Company, Inc.,
1350 Avenue of the Americas,
New York, NY 10019.
Printed in Singapore by
Kim Hup Lee Printing Co. Pte. Ltd.
First Edition
10 9 8 7 6 5 4 3 2 1

Library of Congress
Cataloging-in-Publication Data
Stevenson, James (date)
Sweet corn / by James Stevenson.
    p.   cm.
Summary: A collection of short
poems with titles such as
"Screen Door," "Bike Rental,"
and "Photo Album."
ISBN 0-688-12647-2
1. Children's poetry, American.
[1. American poetry.]
I. Title.   PS3569.T4557S94
1995   811'.54—dc20
94-4902   CIP   AC

FOR AVA

Contents

WHY AM I HAPPY
THAT I WAS BORN?

JUST ONE REASON
(IN SEASON):

SWEET CORN!

There's a tree house
   Up in the apple tree,
A platform of planks
Jammed between the branches.
To get there,
Climb a stairway of sticks
Nailed to the trunk
Like a busted xylophone.
Mountaineers and pirates
Ascend and descend,
Busy as inchworms.

How many are up there now?
It's anybody's guess:
Green leaves keep it secret.
Could be no one, could be three.
Could be ten
With peanut butter
sandwiches
And an excellent
view of France.

If you started with sap green,
Added raw umber,
Maybe some violet,
You might get the sky.

For the sea you'd need cobalt,
Alizarin Crimson,
Possibly ochre,
Ultramarine.

But the faraway ferryboat
Slicing between them,
White as a snowflake
Against a black tree trunk,

They can't make that color.
So leave it plain paper.
Then darken the sky
And darken the sea.

Cows mostly
Seldom climb
Don't travel
Like to

stand there,
mountains,
widely,
stay home.

t the side of the road a man sells old windows,

Hundreds of windows, losing their paint.

They lean every which way,

Stacked against tree trunks.

The man looks as old as the windows he sells.

At times you don't see him . . . he's lost in the sunlight,

Waist-high in diamonds, half-sunk in ice.

He'll sell you a window.

Then when you look through it,

Decide for yourself which is indoors or out.

BIG KIDS

ALWAYS SIT IN

LITTLE KIDS

BIG

KIDS

SEE WHAT'S

LITTLE KIDS NEVER SEE

THE FRONT SEAT

GET STUCK IN THE BACK

COMING

ANYTHING TILL IT'S OVER

Early in the rainy morning
My fat black dog
Rolls off the sofa,
Ambles to the doorway and,
Using her flat forehead
    as a battering ram,
Hits the bottom left corner
    of the screen door,
Sends it flying open—crash!

She walks out onto the porch,
Toenails clicking on the boards.
The screen door slams
    behind her,
A cannon announcing dawn.
Picking a good observation post,
She settles down
    on the wet wood
And takes command of the day.

If there's something you want,

This store doesn't have it.

Well, maybe they have it,

But somebody put it

Over or under some place

Where they lost it.

They say they could get it

(But not very soon).

When the rain has stopped, or you think it has,

And the gutters are dripping on the porch,

You can hear the tiny dancer—

White tie, top hat, gold-tipped cane—

Spattering his taps around the boards:

Time-step toe-drop shuffle brush hop.

Then the sun—

scuff scoot—

Comes out.

Young and old people
Lean over the railings,
Clutching thin strings
That go down to the water.

Maybe they're fishing.
Maybe they're crabbing.
Maybe they're flying their kites
Upside down.

VACANCY/NO VACANCY

POSTCARDS / SOUVENIRS

SALTWATER TAFFY

INDIAN JEWELRY

WATER SLIDE

REPTILE FARM

BANDIT'S CAVE

NATIVE HONEY

RIVER RAFTING

MINI-GOLF

LOOKOUT MOUNTAIN

BAR-B-Q

FALLING ROCKS

WAX MUSEUM

BASEBALL CARDS

VACANCY/NO VACANCY

WHEN THE GOOD

THE THICK DOOR AT

WHITE TRUCK, DRY

INTO THE SUNLIGHT.

FRIGID AIR SWOOP

THAT WAS LOADED

HUMOR MAN OPENED

THE BACK OF HIS

ICE CLOUDS BILLOWED

WE COULD FEEL THE

FROM THE DIM CAVERN

WITH ICE CREAM.

The ladder leaning against the barn

Is like the man who used to use it:

Strong at the beginning,

Okay in the middle,

A few rungs missing at the end.

Across the front of the pale gray woods

Deep red sumac sway on stilts.

Clusters of half-notes

Scribble a crimson score.

When fog blurs the morning,
   Porches glisten, shingles drip.
   Droplets gather on the green screen door.
"Look," they say to one another,
"Look how dry it is inside."

WHEN THE THUNDERSTORM COMES

PUNCHING ITS WAY THROUGH TOWN,

THE DOG STICKS HER NOSE UNDER THE SOFA.

ALL OF US FLINCH AS THE LIGHTNING HITS,

REVEALED AS CRINGING COWARDS IN THE FLASH.

RAIN HURLS ITSELF INTO THE STREET.

THE OLD HOUSE TREMBLES.

BUT EVERYBODY KNOWS

WHEN THIS LETS UP AND THE SKY TURNS BLUE,

WE'LL THROW OUR SNEAKERS OFF AND RACE

TO MUDDY PUDDLES DEEP AND WARM

AND KICK THE WATER BACK INTO THE SKY.

I won't say what I said.

You won't say what you said.

They won't say what they said.

Nobody will cry.

That's the way it will be.

Next time.

Walking the dog on a freezing beach,
I saw two—what? You couldn't call them ships.
Barges? Dredges? Ungainly, eccentric.
The small one a dragon, a dinosaur maybe:
Drill for a nose, hose for a tail,
Two rusty horns sticking into the sky.

The big barge—or dredge—was more like a castle,
A watchtower watching the kingdom of rust.
Bundled-up yeomen preparing odd weapons,
Thinking the dragon might slowly attack?

But what kind of battle could happen between them?
Spitting some mud, and then drifting home?

If I were a king, I'd want this kind of castle.
And next to my castle, a dragon like that.

Free from bedrooms, bathrooms, kitchen,

Flapping, snapping in the breeze,

Only a handful of clothespins

Keeps them from flying

to Spain.

On mornings in August

His store is a table.

To joggers and bikers

He sells lemonade.

But when the sun blazes

And nobody's buying,

He makes an umbrella

Out of his store.

Look at the pictures: Everyone's smiling.
Old friends are posing, giggling and hugging.
Birthdays and weddings, mountains and beaches,
Brothers and sisters, grandmas and babies.
Nobody's angry, nobody's crying,
Nobody's fighting, nobody dies.

Somewhere in the darkrooms
Where pictures get developed,
Sloshed around in chemicals
Beneath a dim red light,
Those other pictures vanished,
Somewhere in the darkness,
Somehow disappeared there,
Never did come out.

Look at the pictures: Everyone's smiling.
Old friends are posing, giggling and hugging.
Birthdays and weddings, mountains and beaches,
Brothers and sisters, grandmas and babies.
Nobody's angry, nobody's crying,
Nobody's fighting, nobody dies.

Rent a bike and go riding.
Rent a pedaling uphill.
Rent a swoop with a view
Of the dunes and the sea.
Rent a whipping past meadows
With wild flowers bending.
Rent a rest in the shade
At the side of the road.

When the rental is over,
They want the bike promptly.
(But what you remember,
They let you take home.)

The backyard's deep in last night's snow.

The dog is sleeping on the sofa.

Her breathing makes a dragging sound:

She may be digging up old bones.

Don't know where they come from,
Don't know where they're going,
People on the bench on the corner of the Green.

Don't know what they're thinking,
Don't know what they're hoping,
People on the bench on the corner of the Green.

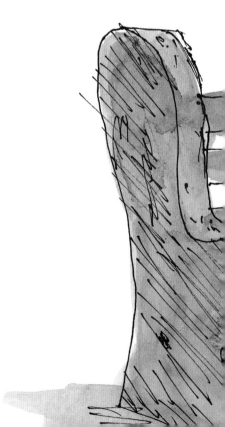

There's the bus departing,
Trailing smoke and fumes. . . .
Just an empty bench on the corner of the Green.

Halfway across,

When both coasts have melted,

A blue balloon's bobbing

On dark choppy waves.

Maybe the wind

Tore the string from cold fingers.

Maybe some child

Thought he'd just

set it

free.

I hope he knows where's he's going,

The old dog trotting along the roadside.

I hope he's going home.

In the dark

Between the trees

The ferryboat goes sliding by,

A ride cut loose

Showing the stars

What light can be.

ablaze,

from a carnival,

For just a few weeks

In unlikely places

Out by the highway, the railroad, the dump,

Watch for the chicory,

Gangly tall chicory,

Lavender butterflies perched on its stalk.

There's never much of it.

Can't take it with you.

Better look quickly, or

Chicory's gone.